MEDITATIONS FROM

Conversations with God, Book 2

Books by Neale Donald Walsch

Conversations with God, Book 1
Conversations with God, Book 2
Conversations with God, Book 1 Guidebook
Meditations from Conversations with God, Book 1

MEDITATIONS FROM
Conversations with God, Book 2
A PERSONAL JOURNAL

Neale Donald Walsch

HAMPTON ROADS
PUBLISHING COMPANY, INC.

Cover design by Marjoram Productions
Cover painting by Louis Jones

For information write:

Hampton Roads Publishing Company, Inc.
134 Burgess Lane
Charlottesville, VA 22902

Or call: (804) 296-2772
FAX: (804) 296-5096

If you are unable to order this book from your local
bookseller, you may order directly from the publisher.
Quantity discounts for organizations are available.
Call 1-800-766-8009, toll-free.

ISBN 1-57174-072-4

10 9 8 7 6 5 4 3 2 1

Printed on acid-free paper in Canada.

Introduction

Throughout all the months that have passed since the initial publication of *Conversations with God* by Hampton Roads in May, 1995, I have been asked one question more than any other: "How," people want to know, "can I have my own conversations with God?"

I have given everyone the same answer. First, get quiet with yourself. Find a time each day for meditation. It doesn't have to be an hour or two. Fifteen minutes will do. Just take some time to be with your SELF. Every day.

Second, try the same technique I use. After you have been in touch with the Quiet Within, write down what comes to you in the moments immediately following. Record what is being given to you by The Silence. Ask a question if you have one, and jot down the answer. Make it the first thing that comes to your mind before you start *thinking* about it.

Now Hampton Roads has provided us all with a tool—a very practical, hands-on tool—with which we might undertake this process, and make it a part of our daily spiritual practice. With this Meditations Journal you will have an opportunity to go within on a daily basis. You'll be able to connect each day with the energies you experienced in *Conversations with God—Book 2*. Use your daily reading of the excerpt to allow yourself to be touched every twenty-four hours with a portion of the wonderful wisdom you found there. Then go within. Look to see what the words you have read mean to you.

Do not be surprised if on a particular day the pre-selected reading seems just right for you—perfect for where you are right then and there. That will probably be the case more often than not. It is the way things work. It is the synergy of the Universe, performing its special magic in your personal world. It is the God and the Goddess walking with you on your path.

Once on that inner path, remain with the quiet; stay with the silence. Be with your Self as long as you can. Then, when your time of silence feels complete, reach again for the Meditations Journal and use the entry space to record a brief conversation with God for the day. If something is bothering you, ask a silent question about it, and write down the answer you receive. Open yourself to the Wisdom Within. Remember, if you do not go within, you go without.

This daily journal can be your sacred space. A place for you to touch, and be touched by, the Divine Intelligence, compassion, and wisdom which *is* the Divine Mother and the Holy Father of all that is. If you use it in that way, this little book can change your life.

Blessed be.
Neale Donald Walsch
Ashland, Oregon
September 10, 1997

MEDITATIONS FROM
Conversations with God, Book 2

. . . we shall never find God so long as *we* are apart. For the first step in finding that we are not apart from God is finding that we are not apart from each other, and until we know and realize that all of *us* are One, we cannot know and realize that we and God are One.

– p. 3

_____

_____

_____

_____

_____

_____

_____

_____

_____

_____

_____

_____

_____

_____

January 2

The fastest way to stop hiding out is to tell the truth. To everyone. All the time. Start telling the truth now, and never stop. Begin by telling the truth to yourself about yourself. Then tell the truth to yourself about another. Then tell the truth about yourself to another. Then tell the truth about another to that other. Finally, tell the truth to everyone about everything.

– p. 3-4

January 3

One *day* of doing nothing but My Will would bring you
Enlightenment.

— p. 5

January 4

Clarity is the first step to mastery.

– p. 7

_____

_____

_____

_____

_____

_____

_____

_____

_____

_____

_____

_____

January 5

I am never *not* with you. You are simply not always *aware*.

– p. 8

_____

_____

_____

_____

_____

_____

_____

_____

_____

_____

_____

_____

_____

_____

January 6

. . . life is an ongoing process of creation.

– p. 10

_____

_____

_____

_____

_____

_____

_____

_____

_____

_____

_____

_____

_____

January 7

The decision you make today is often not the choice you make tomorrow. Yet here is a secret of all Masters: *keep choosing the same thing.*

– p. 10

_____

_____

_____

_____

_____

_____

_____

_____

_____

_____

_____

_____

_____

You can tell you are on your way to mastery when you
see the gap closing between Willing and Experiencing.

— p. 10

_____

_____

_____

_____

_____

_____

_____

_____

_____

_____

_____

_____

_____

_____

January 9

Change your mind all you want. Yet remember that with each change of mind comes a change in the direction of the whole universe.

– p. 10

_____

_____

_____

_____

_____

_____

_____

_____

_____

_____

_____

_____

_____

_____

January 10

When you "make up your mind" about something, you set the universe into motion. Forces beyond your ability to comprehend—far more subtle and complex than you could image—are engaged in a process, the intricate dynamics of which you are only just now beginning to understand.

— p. 11

January 11

Nothing is difficult for Me—but you might be making things very difficult for yourself.

– p. 11

_____

_____

_____

_____

_____

_____

_____

_____

_____

_____

_____

_____

_____

If you choose something, choose it with all your might,
with all your heart. Don't be faint-hearted. Keep going!
Keep moving toward it. Be determined.

– p. 11

_____

_____

_____

_____

_____

_____

_____

_____

_____

_____

_____

_____

_____

January 13

I will "give" you whatever you call forth, whether it's "good" for you or "bad" for you.

— p. 11

_____

_____

_____

_____

_____

_____

_____

_____

_____

_____

_____

_____

_____

_____

January 14

You are a creative being—made in the image and likeness of God.

— p. 12

January 15

You may have whatever you choose. But you may not
have anything you want. In fact, you'll never get *anything*
you want if you want it badly enough.

— p. 12

The moment you say "I want" something, the universe says "Indeed you do" and gives you that precise experience—*the experience of "wanting" it!*

– p. 12

_____

_____

_____

_____

_____

_____

_____

_____

_____

_____

_____

_____

_____

January 17

You call forth precisely what you think, feel, and say.

– p. 12

_____

_____

_____

_____

_____

_____

_____

_____

_____

_____

_____

_____

_____

_____

January 18

There should be only one consideration when making any decision—Is this a statement of Who I Am? Is this an announcement of Who I Choose to Be?

– p. 13

_____

_____

_____

_____

_____

_____

_____

_____

_____

_____

_____

_____

_____

January 19

A life lived by choice is a life of conscious action. A life lived by chance is a life of unconscious reaction.

– p. 13

_____

_____

_____

_____

_____

_____

_____

_____

_____

_____

_____

_____

_____

_____

January 20

When you "re-act," what you do is assess the incoming data, search your memory bank for the same or nearly the same experience, and *act the way you did before.* This is all the work of the mind, not of your soul.

– p. 13

_____

_____

_____

_____

_____

_____

_____

_____

_____

_____

_____

_____

January 21

Your soul would have you search *its* "memory" to see how you might create a truly *genuine experience* of You in the Now Moment. This is the experience of "soul searching" of which you have so often heard, but you have to be literally "out of your mind" to do it.

– p. 13

_____

_____

_____

_____

_____

_____

_____

_____

_____

_____

_____

_____

_____

_____

When you spend your time trying to figure out what's "best" for you, you are doing just that: *spending your time.* Better to *save* your time than to spend it wastefully.

— p. 13

January 23

Remember this: the soul creates, the mind reacts.

– p. 14

_____

_____

_____

_____

_____

_____

_____

_____

_____

_____

_____

_____

_____

_____

January 24

The soul knows in Its wisdom that the experience you are having in This Moment is an experience sent to you by God before you had any conscious awareness of it.

– p. 14

_____

_____

_____

_____

_____

_____

_____

_____

_____

_____

_____

_____

_____

January 25

Every Now Moment is a glorious gift from God.

– p. 14

_____

_____

_____

_____

_____

_____

_____

_____

_____

_____

_____

_____

_____

_____

January 26

The soul intuitively seeks the perfect circumstance and situation now needed to heal wrong thought and bring you the rightful experience of Who You Really Are.

– p. 14

_____

_____

_____

_____

_____

_____

_____

_____

_____

_____

_____

_____

_____

January 27

It is the soul's desire to bring you back to God—to bring you home to Me.

— p. 14

_____

_____

_____

_____

_____

_____

_____

_____

_____

_____

_____

_____

_____

January 28

The soul understands what the mind cannot conceive.

— p. 14

_____

_____

_____

_____

_____

_____

_____

_____

_____

_____

_____

_____

_____

_____

January 29

If you spend your time trying to figure out what's "best" for you, your choices will be cautious, your decisions will take forever, and your journey will be launched on a sea of expectations.

– p. 14

_____

_____

_____

_____

_____

_____

_____

_____

_____

_____

_____

_____

_____

January 30

The soul speaks to you in feelings. Listen to your feelings. Follow your feelings. Honor your feelings.

– p. 14

_____

_____

_____

_____

_____

_____

_____

_____

_____

_____

_____

_____

_____

January 31

Your feelings will *never* get you into "trouble," because your feelings are your *truth*.

— p. 15

_____

_____

_____

_____

_____

_____

_____

_____

_____

_____

_____

_____

_____

_____

February 1

If you listen to your soul you will know what is "best"
for you, because what is best for you is what is true
for you.

_____

_____

_____

_____

_____

_____

_____

_____

_____

_____

_____

_____

_____

February 2

When you act only out of what is true for you, you speed your way down the path. When you *create* an experience based on your "now truth" rather than *react* to an experience based on a "past truth," you produce a "new you."

– p. 15

February 3

Feelings are the language of the soul.

– p. 15

_____

_____

_____

_____

_____

_____

_____

_____

_____

_____

_____

_____

_____

February 4

Feelings are neither negative nor destructive. They are simply truths. How you express your truth is what matters.

– p. 16

_____

_____

_____

_____

_____

_____

_____

_____

_____

_____

_____

_____

_____

_____

February 5

It is not nearly so important how well a message is received as how well it is sent.

– p. 16

_____

_____

_____

_____

_____

_____

_____

_____

_____

_____

_____

_____

_____

February 6

You cannot take responsibility for how well another accepts your truth; you can only ensure how well it is communicated. And by how well, I don't mean merely how clearly; I mean how lovingly, how compassionately, how sensitively, how courageously, and how completely.

– p. 16

_____

_____

_____

_____

_____

_____

_____

_____

_____

_____

_____

_____

_____

_____

_____

February 7

Negativity "kept in" harms the body and burdens the soul.

– p. 16

_____

_____

_____

_____

_____

_____

_____

_____

_____

_____

_____

_____

_____

_____

February 8

Negativity is never a sign of ultimate truth, even if it seems like your truth at the moment.

– p. 17

_____

_____

_____

_____

_____

_____

_____

_____

_____

_____

_____

_____

_____

_____

February 9

The greatest challenge as human beings is to Be Here Now, to stop making things up! Stop creating thoughts about a pre-sent moment (a moment you "sent" yourself *before* you had a thought about it). Be *in the moment*. Remember, you *sent* your Self this moment as a gift.

– p. 18

February 10

. . . when you come to each moment cleanly, *without a previous thought about it*, you can *create* who you *are*, rather than *re-enact* who you *once were*.

– p. 18

_____

_____

_____

_____

_____

_____

_____

_____

_____

_____

_____

_____

February 11

Life is a process of creation, and you keep living it as if it were a process of re-enactment!

– p. 18

_____

_____

_____

_____

_____

_____

_____

_____

_____

_____

_____

_____

_____

_____

February 12

Nothing is more natural than love.

– p. 19

_____

_____

_____

_____

_____

_____

_____

_____

_____

_____

_____

_____

_____

_____

February 13

If you act lovingly, you will be acting naturally.

– p. 19

February 14

You have come to this world in this way, at this time, in this place, to Know Who You Are—and to create Who You Wish to Be.

– p. 19

_____

_____

_____

_____

_____

_____

_____

_____

_____

_____

_____

_____

_____

_____

February 15

Life is an ongoing, never-ending process of re-creation. You keep recreating your selves in the image of your next highest idea about yourselves.

– p. 19

_____

_____

_____

_____

_____

_____

_____

_____

_____

_____

_____

_____

_____

_____

_____

Jesus . . . demonstrated Godliness by demonstrating Unity—and seeing Unity and Wholeness wherever (and upon whomever) he looked. In this his consciousness and My consciousness were One, and, in such a state, whatever he called forth was made manifest in his Divine Reality in that Holy Moment.

— p. 22

_____

_____

_____

_____

_____

_____

_____

_____

_____

_____

_____

_____

_____

_____

Many have been Christed, not just Jesus of Nazareth. *You* can be Christed, too.

– p. 22

February 18

You still think your life is about car repairs and telephone bills and what you want out of relationships, that it's about the *dramas* you've created, rather than the *creator* of those dramas.

— p. 23

_____

_____

_____

_____

_____

_____

_____

_____

_____

_____

_____

_____

_____

February 19

Act like Christ, *every minute of every day.*

_____

_____

_____

_____

_____

_____

_____

_____

_____

_____

_____

_____

_____

_____

February 20

I Am the still small voice within which knows which
way to turn, which path to take, which answer to give,
which action to implement, which word to say—which
reality to create if you truly seek communion and unity
with Me.

_____

_____

_____

_____

_____

_____

_____

_____

_____

_____

_____

_____

_____

February 21

I live in you.

– p. 25

_____

_____

_____

_____

_____

_____

_____

_____

_____

_____

_____

_____

_____

_____

February 22

I am with you always, even unto the end of time.

– p. 25

_____

_____

_____

_____

_____

_____

_____

_____

_____

_____

_____

_____

_____

_____

_____

February 23

Each of you has your own construction. Each of you has understood Me—created Me—in your own way. To some of you I am a man. To some of you I am a woman. To some, I am both. To some, I am neither. To some of you I am pure energy. To some, the ultimate feeling, which you call love. And some of you have no idea what I am. You simply know that I AM.

– p. 25

_____

_____

_____

_____

_____

_____

_____

_____

_____

_____

_____

_____

February 24

I am the beginning of your first thought. I am the end of your last. I am the idea which sparked your most brilliant moment. I am the glory of its fulfillment.

— p. 26

_____

_____

_____

_____

_____

_____

_____

_____

_____

_____

_____

_____

_____

_____

February 25

Whatever works for you, whatever makes if happen—
whatever ritual, ceremony, demonstration, meditation,
thought, song, word, or action it *takes* for you to
"reconnect"—*do this.*

February 26

Stop trying to figure out what is "best" for you (how you can win the most, lose the least, get what you want) and start going with what feels like Who You Are.

– p. 27

_____

_____

_____

_____

_____

_____

_____

_____

_____

_____

_____

_____

_____

_____

_____

February 27

Once you know your truth, *live* it.

– p. 27

_____

_____

_____

_____

_____

_____

_____

_____

_____

_____

_____

_____

_____

February 28

Previous experience is no indicator of truth, since pure Truth is created here and now, not reenacted.

_____

_____

_____

_____

_____

_____

_____

_____

_____

_____

_____

_____

_____

_____

March 1

The past and the future can exist only in thought. The Pre-sent Moment is the Only Reality. *Stay* there! There is no time but *this* time.

_____

_____

_____

_____

_____

_____

_____

_____

_____

_____

_____

_____

_____

_____

March 2

Everything that ever happened, is happening, and ever will happen, is happening right *now* . . . There is only One Moment—*this* moment—the Eternal Moment of Now.

– p. 28-29

_____

_____

_____

_____

_____

_____

_____

_____

_____

_____

_____

_____

_____

March 3

There is no waiting for the glory of God.

_____

_____

_____

_____

_____

_____

_____

_____

_____

_____

_____

_____

_____

_____

There is no Beginning to this, and there is no End. It—the All of Everything —just IS.

— p. 29

March 5

Within the Isness is where your experience—and your greatest secret—lies. You can move in consciousness within the Isness to any "time" or "place" you choose.

– p. 29

_____

_____

_____

_____

_____

_____

_____

_____

_____

_____

_____

_____

_____

March 6

Forever is a right now thing!

– p. 30

March 7

You have always been, are now, and always will be. There has *never* been a time when you were not—nor will there ever *be* such a time.

_____

_____

_____

_____

_____

_____

_____

_____

_____

_____

_____

_____

_____

March 8

Nothing is "older" than *anything*. I created it ALL AT ONCE, and All Of It exists *right now*.

– p. 30

_____

_____

_____

_____

_____

_____

_____

_____

_____

_____

_____

_____

_____

March 9

You are all Aspects of Being, simply parts of What Is. Each part has the consciousness of the Whole imbedded within it. Every element carries the imprint.

– p. 30

_____

_____

_____

_____

_____

_____

_____

_____

_____

_____

_____

_____

_____

March 10

"Awareness" is the experience of that consciousness being awakened. The individual aspect of the ALL becomes aware of Itself. It becomes, quite literally, *self conscious.*

– p. 30

_____

_____

_____

_____

_____

_____

_____

_____

_____

_____

_____

_____

_____

_____

March 11

There *is* no evil!

– p. 31

_____

_____

_____

_____

_____

_____

_____

_____

_____

_____

_____

_____

_____

_____

March 12

You are perfect, just as you are.

– p. 31

_____

_____

_____

_____

_____

_____

_____

_____

_____

_____

_____

_____

_____

_____

A tree is no less perfect because it is a seedling. A tiny infant is no less perfect than a grown-up. It is *perfection itself*. Because it cannot *do* a thing, does not *know* a thing, that does not make it somehow less perfect.

— p. 31

If there are *exceptions* to a rule, then it is not a *rule*.

– p. 32

_____

_____

_____

_____

_____

_____

_____

_____

_____

_____

_____

_____

_____

_____

You cannot hold in "you," because you are as boundless as the Universe. Yet you can create a *concept* about your boundless self by imagining, and then accepting, *boundaries*.

– p. 33

March 16

God is everywhere. Therefore, God is nowhere in particular, because to be somewhere in particular, God would have to *not be somewhere else*—which is *not possible for* God.

– p. 33

_____

_____

_____

_____

_____

_____

_____

_____

_____

_____

_____

_____

_____

March 17

There is only one thing that is "not possible" for God, and that is for God *to not be God.*

– p. 33

_____

_____

_____

_____

_____

_____

_____

_____

_____

_____

_____

_____

_____

_____

March 18

I am everywhere, and that's all there is to it. And since I am everywhere, I am nowhere. And if I am NOWHERE, where am I? NOW HERE.

– p. 33

_____

_____

_____

_____

_____

_____

_____

_____

_____

_____

_____

_____

_____

_____

. . . there are *no* "rotten apples." There are only people who *disagree with your point of view on things*, people who construct a different model of the world.

– p. 34-35

_____

_____

_____

_____

_____

_____

_____

_____

_____

_____

_____

_____

_____

_____

March 20

No persons do anything inappropriate, given their model of the world.

– p. 35

_____

_____

_____

_____

_____

_____

_____

_____

_____

_____

_____

_____

_____

_____

March 21

. . . a definition of "right" and "wrong" is a definition established not only by time, but also by simple geography.

– p. 35

_____

_____

_____

_____

_____

_____

_____

_____

_____

_____

_____

_____

_____

A thing is not intrinsically right or wrong. A thing simply *is*.

– p. 36

_____

_____

_____

_____

_____

_____

_____

_____

_____

_____

_____

_____

_____

March 23

. . . at the moment of your death you will realize the greatest freedom, the greatest peace, the greatest joy, and the greatest love you have ever known.

— p. 36

_____

_____

_____

_____

_____

_____

_____

_____

_____

_____

_____

_____

_____

March 24

Life is not a school, and your purpose here is not to learn; it is to re-member.

– p. 37

_____

_____

_____

_____

_____

_____

_____

_____

_____

_____

_____

_____

_____

_____

March 25

Every event is an Act of God.

– p. 37

_____

_____

_____

_____

_____

_____

_____

_____

_____

_____

_____

_____

_____

_____

March 26

. . . it is *not* My Will that you be punished unceasingly, unendingly, if you do not make the choice I want you to make.

– p. 38

_____

_____

_____

_____

_____

_____

_____

_____

_____

_____

_____

_____

_____

_____

March 27

In your reality, Good cannot exist without Bad. So you believe it must be the same in Mine. Yet I tell you this: There *is* no "bad" where I Am. And there is no Evil. There is only the All of Everything. The Oneness. And the Awareness, the Experience, of that.

— p. 40

_____

_____

_____

_____

_____

_____

_____

_____

_____

_____

_____

_____

March 28

Mine is the place where All There Is is Love.

– p. 40

_____

_____

_____

_____

_____

_____

_____

_____

_____

_____

_____

_____

_____

_____

_____

March 29

There is no "death." Life goes on forever and ever. Life Is. You simply change form.

_____

_____

_____

_____

_____

_____

_____

_____

_____

_____

_____

_____

_____

After you change form, consequences cease to exist.

— p. 40

_____

_____

_____

_____

_____

_____

_____

_____

_____

_____

_____

_____

_____

_____

March 31

In that realm you will know at last the Good News: that your "devil" does not exist, that you are who you always thought you were—goodness and love.

– p. 40

_____

_____

_____

_____

_____

_____

_____

_____

_____

_____

_____

_____

April 1

Others have judged you, and from their judgments you have judged yourself. Now you want God to judge you, and I will not do it.

– p. 41

_____

_____

_____

_____

_____

_____

_____

_____

_____

_____

_____

_____

_____

_____

April 2

... the purpose of life is not to please God. The purpose of life is to know, and to recreate, Who You Are.

– p. 41

_____

_____

_____

_____

_____

_____

_____

_____

_____

_____

_____

_____

_____

April 3

No one who has experienced death *ever mourns the death of anyone.*

– p. 42

_____

_____

_____

_____

_____

_____

_____

_____

_____

_____

_____

_____

_____

April 4

When you see the utter perfection in everything—not just those things with which you agree, but (and perhaps especially) those things with which you disagree—you achieve mastery.

— p. 42

_____

_____

_____

_____

_____

_____

_____

_____

_____

_____

_____

_____

_____

April 5

Every day is sanctified. Every *minute* is holy.

– p. 46

Time is not a continuum. It is an aspect of Relativity that exists in an "up and down" paradigm, with "moments" or "events" stacked on top of each other, happening or occurring at the same "time."

— p. 48

_____

_____

_____

_____

_____

_____

_____

_____

_____

_____

_____

_____

_____

April 7

We are constantly traveling between realities in this realm of time—no time—all time, usually in our sleep.

– p. 48

_____

_____

_____

_____

_____

_____

_____

_____

_____

_____

_____

_____

_____

_____

April 8

The concept of "Age" as it relates to souls really has
to do with levels of awareness, not length of "time."

— p. 48

_____

_____

_____

_____

_____

_____

_____

_____

_____

_____

_____

_____

_____

April 9

All events, all experiences, have as their purpose the creating of *opportunity*.

– p. 49

_____

_____

_____

_____

_____

_____

_____

_____

_____

_____

_____

_____

_____

_____

April 10

Consciousness creates experience.

– p. 49

_____

_____

_____

_____

_____

_____

_____

_____

_____

_____

_____

_____

_____

_____

April 11

*No one comes to you by accident. There is no such thing
as coincidence. Nothing occurs at random. Life is not a
product of chance.* Events, like people, are drawn to you,
by you, for your own purposes.

— p. 50

_____

_____

_____

_____

_____

_____

_____

_____

_____

_____

_____

_____

_____

_____

April 12

Larger planetary experiences and developments are the result of group consciousness. They are drawn to your group as a whole as a result of the choices and desires of the group as a whole.

— p. 50

_____

_____

_____

_____

_____

_____

_____

_____

_____

_____

_____

_____

_____

_____

April 13

If you cannot find a group whose consciousness matches your own, be the *source* of one. Others of like consciousness will be drawn to you.

– p. 50

_____

_____

_____

_____

_____

_____

_____

_____

_____

_____

_____

_____

_____

_____

April 14

Your world, and the condition it is in, is a reflection of the total, combined consciousness of everyone living there.

– p. 51

April 15

Most people define "wrong" as that which is different from them.

– p. 51

_____

_____

_____

_____

_____

_____

_____

_____

_____

_____

_____

_____

_____

April 16

The inability to experience the suffering of another as one's own is what allows such suffering to continue.

– p. 52

April 17

Separation breeds indifference, false superiority. Unity produces compassion, genuine equality.

_____

_____

_____

_____

_____

_____

_____

_____

_____

_____

_____

_____

_____

April 18

Throughout history you have had remarkable teachers, each presenting extraordinary opportunities to remember Who You Really Are. These teachers have shown you the highest and the lowest of the human potential.

– p. 54

April 19

. . . Consciousness is everything, and creates your experience. *Group* consciousness is powerful and produces outcomes of unspeakable beauty or ugliness. The choice is always yours.

– p. 54

_____

_____

_____

_____

_____

_____

_____

_____

_____

_____

_____

_____

_____

April 20

The best way to change the consciousness of others is by your example.

– p. 54

_____

_____

_____

_____

_____

_____

_____

_____

_____

_____

_____

_____

_____

April 21

It begins with *you*. Everything. All things.

– p. 54

_____

_____

_____

_____

_____

_____

_____

_____

_____

_____

_____

_____

_____

_____

_____

April 22

You want the world to change? Change things in your own world.

– p. 54

_____

_____

_____

_____

_____

_____

_____

_____

_____

_____

_____

_____

_____

April 23

When the pain is "ours," not just "yours," when the joy is "ours," not just "mine," when the *whole life experience* is Ours, then it is at last truly that—a Whole Life experience.

— p. 55

_____

_____

_____

_____

_____

_____

_____

_____

_____

_____

_____

_____

_____

April 24

. . . people of both high and low consciousness walk among you—even as *you* walk among others. Which consciousness do you take with you?

– p. 55-56

_____

_____

_____

_____

_____

_____

_____

_____

_____

_____

_____

_____

_____

April 25

First, understand that death is not an end, but a beginning; not a horror, but a joy. It is not a closing down, but an opening up.

– p. 56

_____

_____

_____

_____

_____

_____

_____

_____

_____

_____

_____

_____

_____

_____

April 26

. . . God's love and God's compassion, God's wisdom and God's forgiveness, God's intention and God's *purpose*, are large enough to include the most heinous crime and the most heinous criminal.

_____

_____

_____

_____

_____

_____

_____

_____

_____

_____

_____

_____

_____

_____

April 27

A true understanding of time allows you to live much more peacefully within your reality of relativity, where time is experienced as a movement, a flow, rather than a constant.

– p. 58-59

_____

_____

_____

_____

_____

_____

_____

_____

_____

_____

_____

_____

_____

April 28

It is *you* who are moving, not time.

– p. 59

_____

_____

_____

_____

_____

_____

_____

_____

_____

_____

_____

_____

_____

_____

April 29

Everything that's ever happened—and is ever *going* to happen—is happening *now*.

— p. 62

_____

_____

_____

_____

_____

_____

_____

_____

_____

_____

_____

_____

_____

April 30

You are always at a place of free will and total choice. Being able to see into the "future" (or get others to do it for you) should enhance your ability to live the life you want, not limit it.

— p. 63

_____

_____

_____

_____

_____

_____

_____

_____

_____

_____

_____

_____

_____

If you "see" a future event or experience you do not like, don't *choose* it! Choose again! Select another! Change or alter your behavior so as to *avoid the undesired outcome.*

— p. 63

_____

_____

_____

_____

_____

_____

_____

_____

_____

_____

_____

_____

_____

_____

May 2

You are a Divine Being, capable of more than one experience at the same "time"—and able to divide your Self into as many different "selves" as you choose.

– p. 65

_____

_____

_____

_____

_____

_____

_____

_____

_____

_____

_____

_____

_____

May 3

You are using all of Life—all of *many* lives—to be and *decide* Who You Really Are; to choose and to create Who You Really Are; to experience and to fulfill your current idea about yourself.

— p. 66

_____

_____

_____

_____

_____

_____

_____

_____

_____

_____

_____

_____

May 4

You are in an Eternal Moment of Self creation and Self fulfillment through the process of Self expression.

– p. 66

_____

_____

_____

_____

_____

_____

_____

_____

_____

_____

_____

_____

_____

May 5

This process of creation and recreation is ongoing, never ending, and multi-layered. It is all happening "right now" and on many levels.

– p. 66

_____

_____

_____

_____

_____

_____

_____

_____

_____

_____

_____

_____

_____

May 6

Embrace the Process, and move through it with peace and wisdom and joy. Use the Process, and transform it from something you *endure* to something you *engage* as a tool in the creation of the most magnificent experience of All Time: the fulfillment of your Divine Self.

– p. 67

_____

_____

_____

_____

_____

_____

_____

_____

_____

_____

_____

_____

_____

May 7

Do not waste the precious moments of this, your present reality, seeking to unveil all of life's secrets.

– p. 67

_____

_____

_____

_____

_____

_____

_____

_____

_____

_____

_____

_____

_____

_____

_____

_____

May 8

Decide Who You Are—Who you *want* to be—and then do everything in your power to *be* that.

– p. 67

_____

_____

_____

_____

_____

_____

_____

_____

_____

_____

_____

_____

_____

_____

May 9

If an impression comes to you about the "future," *honor* it. If an idea comes to you about a "past life," see if it has any use for you—don't simply ignore it. Most of all, if a way is made known to you to create, display, express, and experience your Divine Self in ever more glory right here, right now, *follow* that way.

— p. 67

_____

_____

_____

_____

_____

_____

_____

_____

_____

_____

_____

_____

_____

. . . a way *will* be made known to you, because you have asked.

— p. 67

_____

_____

_____

_____

_____

_____

_____

_____

_____

_____

_____

_____

_____

Everyone is creating everything now being experienced — which is another way of saying that *I* am creating everything now being experienced, for *I am everyone.*

– p. 68

_____

_____

_____

_____

_____

_____

_____

_____

_____

_____

_____

_____

_____

May 12

THERE IS ONLY ONE OF US.

– p. 68

May 13

In truth there is no such thing as space—pure, "empty" space, with nothing in it. Everything is *something*.

– p. 69

_____

_____

_____

_____

_____

_____

_____

_____

_____

_____

_____

_____

_____

_____

Your *thoughts* are pure vibration—and they can and *do* create physical matter! If enough of you hold the same thought, you can impact, and even create, portions of your physical universe.

— p. 70

_____

_____

_____

_____

_____

_____

_____

_____

_____

_____

_____

_____

_____

_____

. . . you will *always exist*. You cannot *not* exist. You *are* that which *Is*.

— p. 71

_____

_____

_____

_____

_____

_____

_____

_____

_____

_____

_____

_____

_____

_____

May 16

Understanding about the life of the universe will help you to understand about the life of the universe inside *you*.

– p. 71

_____

_____

_____

_____

_____

_____

_____

_____

_____

_____

_____

_____

_____

May 17

All things move cyclically. There is a natural rhythm to life, and everything moves to that rhythm; everything goes with that flow.

– p. 71

_____

_____

_____

_____

_____

_____

_____

_____

_____

_____

_____

_____

_____

May 18

Few people understand the rhythms of life more than women. Women live their whole lives by rhythm. They are *in* rhythm with life itself.

– p. 72

May 19

Part of the glorious rhythm of life is the yin and the yang. One Aspect of "Being" is not "more perfect" or "better" than another.

– p. 72

_____

_____

_____

_____

_____

_____

_____

_____

_____

_____

_____

_____

_____

_____

You can Be what you wish to Be, choose what you wish to experience. In this lifetime or the next, or the next after that—just as you did in the lifetime before. Each of you is always at choice. Each of you is made up of All of It.

– p. 73

May 21

There is male and female in each of you. Express and experience that aspect of you which it pleases you to express and experience.

– p. 73

_____

_____

_____

_____

_____

_____

_____

_____

_____

_____

_____

_____

_____

_____

May 22

Yet I tell you this: love, love, *love* the things you desire—for your love of them *draws them to you. These things are the stuff of life.* When you love them, you love *life!*

— p. 76

. . . do not choose sex instead of love, *but as a celebration of it.* And do not choose power over, *but power with.* And do not choose fame as an end in itself, *but as a means to a larger end.* And do not choose success at the expense of others, *but as a tool with which to assist others.* And do not choose winning at any cost, *but winning that costs others nothing,* and even brings *them gain as well.*

– p. 76

_____

_____

_____

_____

_____

_____

_____

_____

_____

_____

_____

_____

_____

_____

And by all means choose to KNOW GOD. In fact, CHOOSE THIS FIRST, and all else will follow.

— p. 77

_____

_____

_____

_____

_____

_____

_____

_____

_____

_____

_____

_____

_____

May 25

All of your life you have been taught that it is better to give than to receive. *Yet you cannot give what you do not have. . . . Give yourself abundant pleasure, and you will have abundant pleasure to give others.*

– p. 77

_____

_____

_____

_____

_____

_____

_____

_____

_____

_____

_____

_____

_____

May 26

The more pleasure you give yourself, the more pleasure you can give to another. Likewise, if you give yourself the pleasure of power, you have more power to share with others. The same is true of fame, wealth, glory, success, or anything else which makes you feel good.

— p. 79

_____

_____

_____

_____

_____

_____

_____

_____

_____

_____

_____

_____

_____

May 27

"Feeling good" is the soul's way of shouting "This is who I am!"

– p. 79

. . . no kind of evolution ever took place through *denial*. If you are to evolve, it will not be because you've been able to successfully *deny* yourself the things that you *know* "feel good" but because you've *granted* yourself these pleasures—and found something even greater. For how can you know that something is "greater" if you've never tasted the "lesser"?

– p. 79

May 29

Religion asks you to learn from the experience of others.
Spirituality urges you to seek your own.

– p. 80

_____

_____

_____

_____

_____

_____

_____

_____

_____

_____

_____

_____

_____

Spirituality invites you to toss *away* the thoughts of others and come *up* with your own.

– p. 80

May 31

"Feeling good" is your way of telling yourself that your last thought was *truth*, that your last word was *wisdom*, that your last action was *love*.

_____

_____

_____

_____

_____

_____

_____

_____

_____

_____

_____

_____

_____

June 1

Self-denial is self-destruction.

– p. 80

_____

_____

_____

_____

_____

_____

_____

_____

_____

_____

_____

_____

June 2

Regulating one's behavior is an *active choice* to do or not do something based on one's decision regarding who they are.

— p. 80

_____

_____

_____

_____

_____

_____

_____

_____

_____

_____

_____

_____

_____

_____

June 3

When you come from "we are all One," it is virtually impossible to find that hurting another "feels good."

– p. 81

_____

_____

_____

_____

_____

_____

_____

_____

_____

_____

_____

_____

_____

June 4

. . . grant yourself permission to have *all* that life has to offer—and you will discover it has *more to offer than you've ever imagined.*

– p. 81

_____

_____

_____

_____

_____

_____

_____

_____

_____

_____

_____

_____

_____

_____

June 5

You are what you experience.

– p. 81

_____

_____

_____

_____

_____

_____

_____

_____

_____

_____

_____

_____

_____

June 6

Sexual expression is the inevitable result of an eternal process of attraction and rhythmic energy flow which fuels all of life.

– p. 82

_____

_____

_____

_____

_____

_____

_____

_____

_____

_____

_____

_____

_____

_____

June 7

You are sending off energy—emitting energy—right now, from the center of your being in all direction. This energy—which is *you*—moves outward in wave patterns. The energy leaves you, moves through walls, over mountains, past the moon, and into Forever. It *never, ever stops*.

– p. 82

_____

_____

_____

_____

_____

_____

_____

_____

_____

_____

_____

_____

_____

_____

June 8

You see beauty where you desire to see it. You see ugliness where you are afraid to see beauty.

June 9

Every*one* and every*thing* on the planet—and in the universe—is emitting energy in every direction. This energy mixes with all other energies, criss-crossing in patterns of complexity beyond the ability of your most powerful computers to analyze. The criss-crossing, intermingling, intertwining energies racing between everything that you call physical is what *holds physicality together*.

— p. 87

_____

_____

_____

_____

_____

_____

_____

_____

_____

_____

_____

_____

_____

Thoughts *do* create physical form—and when many people are thinking the *same* thing, there is a very high likelihood their thoughts will form a Reality.

— p. 88

_____

_____

_____

_____

_____

_____

_____

_____

_____

_____

_____

_____

_____

June 11

What made American great was not that every man struggled for his *own* survival, but that every man accepted individual responsibility for the survival of *all*.

– p. 89

_____

_____

_____

_____

_____

_____

_____

_____

_____

_____

_____

_____

_____

_____

_____

June 12

Each person *must* take responsibility for herself or himself—that is undeniably true. But America—and your world—can truly work only when every person is willing to stand responsible for *all* of you as a *Whole*.

_____

_____

_____

_____

_____

_____

_____

_____

_____

_____

_____

_____

_____

June 13

. . . for God to *know* Itself as the All of It, God must know Itself as *not* the All of It.

– p. 91

June 14

For God *is* the All, and the Goddess is *everything*, and there is nothing else that is; and all that *ever* was, is *now*, and ever *shall* be, is your world without end.

— p. 92

_____

_____

_____

_____

_____

_____

_____

_____

_____

_____

_____

_____

_____

June 15

Lack of privacy does not equal lack of sanctity. Most of humanity's most sacred rites are performed in public.

– p. 94

_____

_____

_____

_____

_____

_____

_____

_____

_____

_____

_____

_____

_____

June 16

The trouble with "propriety" is that someone has to set the standards. This means, automatically, that your behaviors are being limited, directed, *dictated* by someone *else's* idea of what should bring you joy.

– p. 95

_____

_____

_____

_____

_____

_____

_____

_____

_____

_____

_____

_____

_____

June 17

Not just in matters of sexuality, but in all of life, never, ever, *ever*, fail to do something simply because it might violate someone's *else's* standards of propriety.

– p. 95

_____

_____

_____

_____

_____

_____

_____

_____

_____

_____

_____

_____

_____

June 18

"Propriety" had nothing to do with your relative values of "rightness" or "wrongness."

– p. 95

_____

_____

_____

_____

_____

_____

_____

_____

_____

_____

_____

_____

_____

_____

June 19

"Appropriate" behavior is not always the behavior that's in what you call your "best interests." It is rarely the behavior that brings you the most joy.

– p. 96

_____

_____

_____

_____

_____

_____

_____

_____

_____

_____

_____

_____

_____

June 20

The central question in ANY decision is, "What would love do now?"

– p. 96

_____

_____

_____

_____

_____

_____

_____

_____

_____

_____

_____

_____

_____

_____

_____

June 21

If you love another, you will not do anything that you believe could or would hurt that person.

– p. 96

_____

_____

_____

_____

_____

_____

_____

_____

_____

_____

_____

_____

June 22

Betrayal of yourself in order not to betray another is Betrayal nonetheless. It is the Highest Betrayal.

June 23

You assume that man will always make what you call
the "selfish choice." I tell you this: Man *is* capable of
making the *highest* choice. Yet I also tell you this: The
Highest Choice is not *always* the choice which seems
to serve another.

– p. 97

_____

_____

_____

_____

_____

_____

_____

_____

_____

_____

_____

_____

_____

_____

June 24

When your purpose—your *life* purpose—is very high, so will your choices also be. Putting yourself first does not mean being what you term "selfish"—it means being self *aware*.

– p. 98

June 25

It is only through the exercise of the greatest freedom that the greatest growth is achieved—or even possible. If all you are doing is following someone *else's* rules, then you have not grown, you have obeyed.

– p. 98

_____

_____

_____

_____

_____

_____

_____

_____

_____

_____

_____

_____

June 26

Are you nurturing your soul? Are you even *noticing* it?
Are you healing it or hurting it? Are you growing or
withering? Are you expanding or contracting?

– p. 100

_____

_____

_____

_____

_____

_____

_____

_____

_____

_____

_____

_____

_____

June 27

. . . when was the last time you felt your soul being *expressed*? When was the last time you cried with joy? Wrote poetry? Made music? Danced in the rain? Baked a pie? Painted *anything*? . . . Swam naked? Walked at sunrise? Played the harmonica? Talked 'til dawn? Made love for hours . . . on a beach, in the woods? Communed with nature? Searched for God?

— p. 100

_____

_____

_____

_____

_____

_____

_____

_____

_____

_____

_____

_____

_____

_____

When you live as a three-part being, you come at last into balance with yourself. Your concerns include matters of the soul: spiritual identity; life purpose; relationship to God; path of evolution; spiritual growth; ultimate destiny.

– p. 100

_____

_____

_____

_____

_____

_____

_____

_____

_____

_____

_____

_____

_____

_____

June 29

As you evolve into higher and higher states of consciousness, you bring into full realization every aspect of your being. Yet evolution does not mean *dropping* some aspects of Self in favor of others. It simply means expanding focus; turning away from almost exclusive involvement with one aspect, toward genuine love and appreciation for *all* aspects.

– p. 101

_____

_____

_____

_____

_____

_____

_____

_____

_____

_____

_____

_____

_____

June 30

Appreciation for *all* of life is what honors the Process I have created. Disdain for life or any of its joys—even the most basic, physical ones—is disdain for *Me*, the Creator. For when you call My creation unholy, what do you call Me? Yet when you call My creation sacred, you sanctify your experience of it, and Me as well.

– p. 102

_____

_____

_____

_____

_____

_____

_____

_____

_____

_____

_____

_____

_____

July 1

. . . nothing is disapproved of by God. I do not sit here
in judgment, calling one action *Good* and another *Evil*.

– p. 102

_____

_____

_____

_____

_____

_____

_____

_____

_____

_____

_____

_____

_____

_____

July 2

No action which causes hurt to another leads to rapid evolution.

– p. 102

_____

_____

_____

_____

_____

_____

_____

_____

_____

_____

_____

_____

_____

_____

_____

July 3

No action involving another may be taken without the other's agreement and permission.

— p. 103

_____

_____

_____

_____

_____

_____

_____

_____

_____

_____

_____

_____

_____

July 4

Whether it's loveless sex or loveless spaghetti and meatballs, if you've prepared the feast and are consuming it without love, you're missing the most extraordinary part of the experience.

– p. 103

_____

_____

_____

_____

_____

_____

_____

_____

_____

_____

_____

_____

_____

_____

July 5

Children are aware of themselves as sexual beings—
which is to say, as *human* beings—from the outset of
their lives. What many parents on your planet now do
is try to discourage them from noticing that.

— p. 104

_____

_____

_____

_____

_____

_____

_____

_____

_____

_____

_____

_____

July 6

With your race of beings, it has not been a question of when you introduce your offspring to sex, it has been a question of when you stop demanding that they deny their own identity as sexual beings.

— p. 104

July 7

Stop teaching children from the very beginning of their lives that things having to do with the very natural functioning of their bodies are shameful and wrong.

– p. 106

_____

_____

_____

_____

_____

_____

_____

_____

_____

_____

_____

_____

_____

_____

July 8

Allow your children to see and observe the romantic side of *you*. Let them see you hugging, touching, gently fondling—let them see that their parents *love each other* and that *showing their love physically* is something that is very natural and very wonderful.

_____

_____

_____

_____

_____

_____

_____

_____

_____

_____

_____

_____

_____

_____

July 9

When your children begin to embrace their own sexual feelings, curiosities and urges, cause them to connect this new and expanding experience of themselves with an inner sense of joy and celebration, not guilt and shame.

— p. 106

_____

_____

_____

_____

_____

_____

_____

_____

_____

_____

_____

_____

_____

July 10

Children think their parents are asexual because their parents have *portrayed themselves that way*. They then imagine that they must be this way, because *all children emulate their parents*.

– p. 107

July 11

So talk about sex with your children, laugh about sex with your children, teach them and allow them and remind them and *show them how to celebrate* their sexuality.

— p. 107

_____

_____

_____

_____

_____

_____

_____

_____

_____

_____

_____

_____

. . . discover, revisit, regain, reclaim your *own* sexuality. Celebrate *that*. Enjoy *that*. Own *that*. Own your own joyful sexuality, and then you can allow and encourage your children to own theirs.

— p. 108

_____

_____

_____

_____

_____

_____

_____

_____

_____

_____

_____

_____

_____

_____

July 13

Enjoy everything. Need nothing . . . Needing someone is the fastest way to kill a relationship . . . the greatest gift you can give someone is the strength and the power *not to need you*, to need you for nothing.

– p. 108

_____

_____

_____

_____

_____

_____

_____

_____

_____

_____

_____

_____

_____

July 14

Most of the human race has decided that the meaning and the purpose and the function of education is to pass on knowledge; that to educate someone is to give them knowledge—generally, the accumulated knowledge of one's particular family, clan, tribe, society, nation, and world. Yet education has very little to do with knowledge.

– p. 110

_____

_____

_____

_____

_____

_____

_____

_____

_____

_____

_____

_____

July 15

Wisdom is knowledge applied.

– p. 110

_____

_____

_____

_____

_____

_____

_____

_____

_____

_____

_____

_____

_____

_____

July 16

When you give your children wisdom, you do not tell them what to know, or what is true, but, rather, *how to get to their own truth.*

July 17

Knowledge is lost. Wisdom is never forgotten.

– p. 111

July 18

Children are taught to *remember* facts and fictions—the fictions each society has set up about itself—rather than given the ability to discover and create their own truths.

– p. 112

_____

_____

_____

_____

_____

_____

_____

_____

_____

_____

_____

_____

_____

_____

July 19

History is supposed to be an accurate, and full, account of what actually happened. Politics is never about what actually happened. Politics is always one's *point of view* about what happened.

– p. 113

_____

_____

_____

_____

_____

_____

_____

_____

_____

_____

_____

_____

_____

_____

July 20

. . . do you really think things were better 30 years ago, 40 years ago, 50 years ago? I say memory has poor vision. You remember the good of it, and not the worst of it. It's natural, it's normal. But don't be deceived. Do some *critical thinking*, and not just *memorizing* what others want you to think.

— p. 116

_____

_____

_____

_____

_____

_____

_____

_____

_____

_____

_____

_____

July 21

You don't *want* your young ones drawing their own conclusions. You want them to *come to the same conclusions you came to*. Thus, you doom them to repeat the mistakes to which your conclusions led *you*.

— p. 117

July 22

You have not allowed your schools to teach that love is all there is. You have not allowed your schools to speak of a love which is unconditional.

– p. 117

_____

_____

_____

_____

_____

_____

_____

_____

_____

_____

_____

_____

_____

_____

July 23

In societies where history is not bent to the views of the strongest and most powerful, the mistakes of the past are openly acknowledged and never repeated, and *once is enough* for behaviors which are clearly self destructive.

– p. 117

_____

_____

_____

_____

_____

_____

_____

_____

_____

_____

_____

_____

_____

July 24

The young people are destroying your way of life. The young people have *always* done that. Your job is to encourage it, not discourage it.

– p. 119

July 25

What you memorize, you memorialize.

– p. 121

_____

_____

_____

_____

_____

_____

_____

_____

_____

_____

_____

_____

July 26

They are spirits, entering a physical body. That is not an easy thing for a spirit to do; not an easy thing for a spirit to get used to. It is very confining, very limiting. So the child will cry out at suddenly being so limited. Hear this cry. Understand it. And give your children as much of a sense of "unlimitedness" as you possibly can.

– p. 121

July 27

. . . introduce them to the world you have created with gentleness and care. Be full of care—that is to say, be careful—of what you put into their memory storage units. Children remember everything they see, everything they experience.

— p. 121

_____

_____

_____

_____

_____

_____

_____

_____

_____

_____

_____

_____

_____

July 28

Why do you not teach your children of movement and music and the joy of art and the mystery of fairy tales and the wonder of life? Why do you not bring out what is naturally found *in* the child, rather than seek to put in what is unnatural to the child?

– p. 122

_____

_____

_____

_____

_____

_____

_____

_____

_____

_____

_____

_____

_____

_____

July 29

... teach *concepts*, not *subjects*. Devise a new curriculum, and build it around three Core Concepts: Awareness, Honesty, Responsibility. Teach your children these concepts from the earliest age. Have them run through the curriculum until the final day. Base your entire educational model upon them. Birth all instruction deep within them.

— p. 122

_____

_____

_____

_____

_____

_____

_____

_____

_____

_____

_____

_____

_____

July 30

Until you are willing to take responsibility for all of it, *you cannot change any of it.*

— p. 125

_____

_____

_____

_____

_____

_____

_____

_____

_____

_____

_____

_____

_____

July 31

You don't know how to solve conflict without violence.
You don't know how to live without fear. You don't
know how to act without self interest. You don't know
how to love without conditions.

— p. 126

_____

_____

_____

_____

_____

_____

_____

_____

_____

_____

_____

_____

Create the grandest version of the greatest vision you ever had about yourselves as a human race. Then, take the values and concepts which undergird such a vision and *teach them in your schools.*

— p. 126

_____

_____

_____

_____

_____

_____

_____

_____

_____

_____

_____

_____

_____

August 2

Right now your schools exist primarily to provide answers. It would be far more beneficial if their primary function was to ask questions.

– p. 128

_____

_____

_____

_____

_____

_____

_____

_____

_____

_____

_____

_____

_____

_____

August 3

Past Data should not be the basis of Present Truth.
Data from a prior time or experience should always
and only be the basis for new questions. Always the
treasure should be in the question, not in the answer.

– p. 128

_____

_____

_____

_____

_____

_____

_____

_____

_____

_____

_____

_____

_____

_____

August 4

Everything in your life has served you, brought you to
this moment.

– p. 129

_____

_____

_____

_____

_____

_____

_____

_____

_____

_____

_____

_____

_____

_____

August 5

No questions are undeserving or unworthy.

— p. 132

_____

_____

_____

_____

_____

_____

_____

_____

_____

_____

_____

_____

_____

August 6

. . . from My standpoint, *nothing* is "wrong.". . .I'll use the term "wrong" to mean "that which is not serving you, given who and what you choose to be." This is how I've always used the terms "right" and "wrong" with you; it is always within this context, for, in truth, there is no Right and Wrong.

– p. 132

_____

_____

_____

_____

_____

_____

_____

_____

_____

_____

_____

_____

_____

August 7

Deception is part of government, for few people would choose to be governed the way they are governed—few would choose to be governed at all—unless government convinced them that its decisions were for their own good.

– p. 133

_____

_____

_____

_____

_____

_____

_____

_____

_____

_____

_____

_____

_____

_____

August 8

Truth and politics do not and *cannot* mix because politics is the *art* of saying only what needs to be said—and saying it in just the right way—in order to achieve a desired end.

– p. 133

_____

_____

_____

_____

_____

_____

_____

_____

_____

_____

_____

_____

August 9

Not all politics are bad, but the art of politics is a *practical* art. It recognizes with great candor the psychology of most people. It simply notices that most people operate out of self-interest. So politics is the way that people of power seek to convince you that *their* self-interest is *your own*.

– p. 133

August 10

When government began to be the people's *provider* as well as the people's protector, governments started *creating* society, rather than preserving it.

— p. 133

_____

_____

_____

_____

_____

_____

_____

_____

_____

_____

_____

_____

_____

August 11

... in providing for people's needs, you must be careful not to rob them of their greatest dignity: the exercise of personal power, individual creativity, and the single-minded ingenuity which allows people to notice that they can provide for themselves.

— p. 134

_____

_____

_____

_____

_____

_____

_____

_____

_____

_____

_____

_____

_____

August 12

You cannot legislate morality. You cannot mandate equality. What is needed is a *shift* of collective consciousness, not an *enforcer* of collective conscience.

– p. 135

_____

_____

_____

_____

_____

_____

_____

_____

_____

_____

_____

_____

_____

_____

August 13

Behavior (and all laws, and all government programs) must spring from Beingness, must be a true reflection of Who You *Are*.

– p. 135

_____

_____

_____

_____

_____

_____

_____

_____

_____

_____

_____

_____

_____

August 14

Generally, nothing serves "the many" more than letting them govern themselves.

– p. 135

_____

_____

_____

_____

_____

_____

_____

_____

_____

_____

_____

_____

_____

August 15

You cannot grow and become great when you are constantly being told what to do by government.

— p. 135

_____

_____

_____

_____

_____

_____

_____

_____

_____

_____

_____

_____

_____

_____

_____

_____

August 16

I am not suggesting a world with no codes of behavior, no agreements. I am suggesting that your agreements and codes be based on a higher understanding and a grander definition of self-interest.

– p. 136

_____

_____

_____

_____

_____

_____

_____

_____

_____

_____

_____

_____

_____

_____

August 17

. . . if providing for the good of the many does not produce a huge profit for someone, the *good of the many is more often than not ignored.*

August 18

The basic question facing humankind, therefore, is: Can self-interest ever be replaced by the best interests, the *common* interest, of humankind? If so, how?

– p. 138

_____

_____

_____

_____

_____

_____

_____

_____

_____

_____

_____

_____

_____

August 19

The entire planet faces a crisis of consciousness. You must decide whether you simply *care for each other*.

– p. 140

_____

_____

_____

_____

_____

_____

_____

_____

_____

_____

_____

_____

_____

_____

August 20

You *do* love the members of your own family. You simply have a very limited view of who your family members *are*. You do not consider yourself part of the human family, and so the problems of the human family are not your own.

– p. 140

_____

_____

_____

_____

_____

_____

_____

_____

_____

_____

_____

_____

_____

_____

August 21

You must begin to see someone else's interests as your own.

– p. 141

_____

_____

_____

_____

_____

_____

_____

_____

_____

_____

_____

_____

_____

_____

August 22

. . . the *only problem of humanity* is lack of love.

– p. 142

August 23

The fastest way to get to a place of love and concern for all humankind is to see all humankind as your *family*. The fastest way to see all humankind as your family is to *stop separating yourself*.

p. 142

August 24

Spiritual truth must be lived in practical life to change everyday experience.

– p. 148

_____

_____

_____

_____

_____

_____

_____

_____

_____

_____

_____

_____

August 25

If you derive your life's greatest happiness from experiences obtainable only in the Outside World—the physical world outside of yourself—you will *never* want to give up an *ounce* of all that you've piled up, as a person and a nation, to make you happy.

– p. 150

_____

_____

_____

_____

_____

_____

_____

_____

_____

_____

_____

_____

_____

_____

August 26

All of *life* is spiritual, and therefore all of life's problems
are spiritually based—and *spiritually solved.*

_____

_____

_____

_____

_____

_____

_____

_____

_____

_____

_____

_____

_____

August 27

All conflict arises from misplaced desire.

– p. 151

_____

_____

_____

_____

_____

_____

_____

_____

_____

_____

_____

_____

_____

August 28

Let each person find peace within. When you find peace within, you also find that you can do without.

– p. 151

_____

_____

_____

_____

_____

_____

_____

_____

_____

_____

_____

_____

_____

_____

"Not needing" is a great freedom. It frees you, first, from fear: fear that there is something you won't have; fear that there is something you have that you will lose; and fear that without a certain thing, you won't be happy.

– p. 151

August 30

Anger is fear announced. When you have nothing to fear, you have nothing over which to be angry.

August 31

When you find Inner Peace, neither the presence nor the absence of any person, place or thing, condition, circumstance, or situation can be the Creator of your state of mind or the cause of your experience of being.

– p. 152

_____

_____

_____

_____

_____

_____

_____

_____

_____

_____

_____

_____

_____

_____

September 1

There is perfection in everything.

– p. 153

September 2

Feel your feelings. Cry your cries. Laugh your laughs. Honor your truth. Yet when all the emotion is done, be still and know that I am God. In other words, in the midst of the greatest tragedy, see the glory of the process.

— p. 153

_____

_____

_____

_____

_____

_____

_____

_____

_____

_____

_____

_____

_____

September 3

In a moment of great tragedy, the challenge always is
to quiet the mind and move deep within the soul.

– p. 153

_____

_____

_____

_____

_____

_____

_____

_____

_____

_____

_____

_____

_____

September 4

There is only one question of any relevance regarding this or any other thought. Does it serve you to hold that? In terms of Who You Are and Who You seek to Be, does that thought serve you?

– p. 156

_____

_____

_____

_____

_____

_____

_____

_____

_____

_____

_____

_____

_____

September 5

. . . at a very high metaphysical level, no one is "disadvantaged," for each soul creates for itself the exact people, events, and circumstances needed to accomplish what It wishes to accomplish.

– p. 156

September 6

Remember first that everything you think, say, and do is a reflection of what you've decided about yourself; a statement of Who You Are; an act of *creation* in your deciding who you want to *be*.

— p. 157

_____

_____

_____

_____

_____

_____

_____

_____

_____

_____

_____

_____

_____

September 7

. . . when you come across a person who appears, in relative terms as observed within your world, to be disadvantaged, the first question you have to ask is: Who am I and who do I choose to *be*, in relationship to that? In other words, the first question when you encounter another in *any* circumstance should always be: What do I want here?

– p. 157

_____

_____

_____

_____

_____

_____

_____

_____

_____

_____

_____

_____

. . .the reason your relationships are in such a mess is that you're always trying to figure out what the other person wants and what other *people* want—instead of what *you* truly want.

— p. 157

September 9

The purpose of your Holy Relationship with every other person, place, or thing is not to figure out what *they* want or need, but what *you* require or desire now in order to *grow*, in order to be Who you *want* to be.

– p. 158

_____

_____

_____

_____

_____

_____

_____

_____

_____

_____

_____

_____

_____

September 10

Consciousness—that of which you are truly aware—is the basis of all truth and thus of all true spirituality.

– p. 159

_____

_____

_____

_____

_____

_____

_____

_____

_____

_____

_____

_____

_____

_____

September 11

Sometimes the best way to love someone, and the most help you can give, is to *leave them alone* or empower them to help themselves.

— p. 159

_____

_____

_____

_____

_____

_____

_____

_____

_____

_____

_____

_____

_____

September 12

Jesus' great gift was that he saw everyone as who they truly are. He refused to accept appearances; he refused to believe what others believed of themselves. He always had a higher thought, and he always invited others *to* it. Yet he also honored where others chose to be. He did not require them to accept his higher idea, merely held it out as an invitation.

— p. 160

_____

_____

_____

_____

_____

_____

_____

_____

_____

_____

_____

_____

_____

_____

September 13

Jesus' idea of Perfect Love was to grant all persons exactly the help they requested, after telling them the kind of help they could *get*.

– p. 161

_____

_____

_____

_____

_____

_____

_____

_____

_____

_____

_____

_____

_____

September 14

For to the extent that you allow other persons to make you responsible for them, to that extent you have allowed them to make you powerful.

– p. 162

September 15

The goal is to help the weak grow strong, not to let the weak become weaker.

– p. 162

September 16

The idea behind the statement "From each according to his ability, to each according to his need" is not evil, it is beautiful. It is simply another way of saying you are your brother's keeper.

– p. 162

_____

_____

_____

_____

_____

_____

_____

_____

_____

_____

_____

_____

_____

September 17

Government is the human attempt to mandate goodness and ensure fairness. Yet there is only one place where goodness is born, and that is in the human heart. There is only one place where fairness can be conceptualized, and that is in the human mind. There is only one place where love can be experienced truly, and that is in the human soul. Because the human soul *is love*.

– p. 166

_____

_____

_____

_____

_____

_____

_____

_____

_____

_____

_____

_____

September 18

But truly, even these basic laws—prohibitions against murdering, damaging, cheating, or even running a red light—shouldn't be needed and *wouldn't* be needed if all people everywhere simply followed the *Laws of Love*. That is, God's Law.

-- p. 167

. . . some level of government is going to be required until your race evolves to the point where you *naturally do* what is *naturally right* . . . The real question is not why do governments impose so many rules and regulations on the people, but why do governments *have* to?

– p. 168

September 20

If every person on the planet had basic needs met—if the mass of the people could live in dignity and escape the struggle of simple survival—would this not open the way for all of humankind to engage in more noble pursuits?

– p. 169

September 21

What kind of glory is obtained when it is achieved at the expense of another?

– p. 169

_____

_____

_____

_____

_____

_____

_____

_____

_____

_____

_____

_____

_____

September 22

If your well-off say they do not want to help the starving and the homeless because they do not want to disempower them, then your well-off are hypocrites. For no one is truly "well off" if they are well off while others are dying.

– p. 169

_____

_____

_____

_____

_____

_____

_____

_____

_____

_____

_____

_____

_____

September 23

The evolution of a society is measured by how well it treats the least among its members.

– p. 169

_____

_____

_____

_____

_____

_____

_____

_____

_____

_____

_____

_____

_____

September 24

When in doubt, always err on the side of compassion.
The test of whether you are helping or hurting: Are
your fellow humans enlarged or reduced as a result of
your help? Have you made them bigger or smaller?
More able or less able?

– p. 170

_____

_____

_____

_____

_____

_____

_____

_____

_____

_____

_____

_____

_____

September 25

Isn't basic human dignity the birthright of everyone?

– p. 170

_____

_____

_____

_____

_____

_____

_____

_____

_____

_____

_____

_____

_____

September 26

The challenge is not to make everyone equal, but to give everyone at least the assurance of basic survival with dignity, so that each may then have the chance to choose what more they want from there.

– p. 170

_____

_____

_____

_____

_____

_____

_____

_____

_____

_____

_____

_____

_____

September 27

Compassion never ends, love never stops, patience never runs out in God's World. Only in the world of man is goodness limited.

— p. 171

_____

_____

_____

_____

_____

_____

_____

_____

_____

_____

_____

_____

_____

September 28

When you throw My goodness back in My face (which, by the way, the human race has done to God for millennia), I see that you are merely *mistaken*. You do not know what is in your best interest. I have compassion because your mistake is based not in evil, but in ignorance.

– p. 171

_____

_____

_____

_____

_____

_____

_____

_____

_____

_____

_____

_____

_____

September 29

. . . all attack is a call for help.

– p. 172

_____

_____

_____

_____

_____

_____

_____

_____

_____

_____

_____

_____

_____

_____

September 30

The change that must be made can be made only in the hearts of men.

– p. 173

_____

_____

_____

_____

_____

_____

_____

_____

_____

_____

_____

_____

_____

October 1

You must stop seeing God as separate from you, and you as separate from each other.

— p. 173

_____

_____

_____

_____

_____

_____

_____

_____

_____

_____

_____

_____

_____

October 2

Love gives all and requires nothing.

– p. 173

October 3

The only reason you require *anything* is because some-one else is holding back.

– p. 174

October 4

Be a light unto the world, and hurt it not. Seek to build, not to destroy.

– p. 175

October 5

Seek only Godliness. Speak only in truthfulness. Act only in love.

– p. 175

October 6

Use every moment to think the highest thought, say the highest word, do the highest deed. In this, glorify your Holy Self, and thus, too, glorify Me.

– p. 175

October 7

Bring peace to the Earth by bringing peace to all those whose lives you touch.

– p. 175

_____

_____

_____

_____

_____

_____

_____

_____

_____

_____

_____

_____

_____

_____

October 8

Feel and express in every moment your Divine Connection with the All, and with every person, place, and thing . . . Be a living, breathing example of the Highest Truth that resides within you.

– p. 175-176

_____

_____

_____

_____

_____

_____

_____

_____

_____

_____

_____

_____

_____

October 9

Make of your life a gift. Remember always, you *are* the gift! Be a gift to everyone who enters your life . . .

– p. 176

_____

_____

_____

_____

_____

_____

_____

_____

_____

_____

_____

_____

_____

October 10

When someone enters your life unexpectedly, *look for the gift that person has come to receive from you.*

– p. 176

_____

_____

_____

_____

_____

_____

_____

_____

_____

_____

_____

_____

_____

_____

October 11

I HAVE SENT YOU NOTHING BUT ANGELS.

– p. 177

_____

_____

_____

_____

_____

_____

_____

_____

_____

_____

_____

_____

_____

_____

_____

October 12

Completely *ignoring* the plight of another who is truly seeking your help is not the answer, for doing too little no more empowers the other than doing too much.

– p. 178

_____

_____

_____

_____

_____

_____

_____

_____

_____

_____

_____

_____

_____

October 13

You are concerned about little on your planet except the satisfying of your own passions, the meeting of your own immediate (and mostly bloated) needs, and quenching the endless human desire for Bigger, Better, More. Yet you might do well as a species to ask, when is enough enough?

– p. 182

_____

_____

_____

_____

_____

_____

_____

_____

_____

_____

_____

_____

_____

October 14

If every*one* knew every*thing* about every*body's* money situation, there would be an uprising in your country and on your planet, the likes of which you have never seen. And in the aftermath of that there would be fairness and equity, honesty and true for-the-good-of-all priority in the conduct of human affairs.

– p. 183

_____

_____

_____

_____

_____

_____

_____

_____

_____

_____

_____

_____

_____

October 15

Nothing breeds appropriate behavior faster than exposure to the light of public scrutiny.

– p. 186

October 16

When the chief aim and goal of your society (as it is in all truly enlightened societies) is the survival of *all*; the benefit, equally, of *all*; the providing of a good life for *all*, then your need for secrecy and quiet dealings and under the table maneuverings and money which can be hidden will disappear.

– p. 188

_____

_____

_____

_____

_____

_____

_____

_____

_____

_____

_____

_____

_____

_____

October 17

... *nothing* breeds fairness faster than *visibility*. *Visibility* is simply another word for *truth*.

– p. 188

_____

_____

_____

_____

_____

_____

_____

_____

_____

_____

_____

_____

_____

_____

October 18

. . . no one in enlightened societies is willing to get *anything*, or *have* anything, at *someone else's expense*.

– p. 189

_____

_____

_____

_____

_____

_____

_____

_____

_____

_____

_____

_____

_____

October 19

. . . the best personal relationships, and certainly the best romantic ones, are relationships in which everyone knows everything; in which *visibility* is not only the watchword, but the *only word*; in which there simply are no secrets.

– p. 189

_____

_____

_____

_____

_____

_____

_____

_____

_____

_____

_____

_____

_____

October 20

Do you think you could live a life like this? No more secrets? Absolute visibility? If not, why not? What are you keeping from others that you don't want them to know? What are you saying to someone that isn't true? What are you not saying to someone that is?

– p. 191

_____

_____

_____

_____

_____

_____

_____

_____

_____

_____

_____

_____

_____

October 21

Each of you has constructed, within the framework of your own particular theology, some idea, some concept of God's Worst Punishment. And I hate to tell you this, because I see the fun you're having with the drama of it all, but, well . . . *just ain't no such thing.*

– p. 192

_____

_____

_____

_____

_____

_____

_____

_____

_____

_____

_____

_____

_____

_____

October 22

Perhaps when you lose the fear of having your life become totally visible at the moment of your death, you can get over the fear of having your life become totally visible *while you are living it.*

October 23

Seek the truth, say the truth, live the truth every day. Do this with yourself and with every person whose life you touch.

– p. 192

_____

_____

_____

_____

_____

_____

_____

_____

_____

_____

_____

_____

_____

_____

October 24

But you don't have to leave the planet or even leave your house to begin experiencing what such a New Thought system would be like. Start in your own family, in your own home. If you own a business, start in your own company.

– p. 193

_____

_____

_____

_____

_____

_____

_____

_____

_____

_____

_____

_____

_____

_____

October 25

Be the new way. Be the higher way. Be the grandest
way. Then you can truly say, *I am the way and the life.*
Follow me.

– p. 194

_____

_____

_____

_____

_____

_____

_____

_____

_____

_____

_____

_____

_____

_____

October 26

If the whole world followed you, would you be pleased with where you took it?

– p. 194

_____

_____

_____

_____

_____

_____

_____

_____

_____

_____

_____

_____

_____

_____

_____

There will always be disagreements between nations, for disagreement is merely a sign—and a healthy one—of individuality. *Violent resolution* of disagreements, however, is a sign of extraordinary immaturity.

– p. 195

_____

_____

_____

_____

_____

_____

_____

_____

_____

_____

_____

_____

_____

October 28

As long as you think you can win an argument, you will have it. As long as you think you can win a war, you will fight it.

– p. 195

_____

_____

_____

_____

_____

_____

_____

_____

_____

_____

_____

_____

_____

_____

October 29

Sometimes the only way to *avoid* a war is to *have* a war. Sometimes you have to do what you don't *want* to do in order to ensure that you won't *have to keep on doing it*!

– p. 196

October 30

. . . often the only way to know yourself as That Which You Are is to experience yourself as That Which You Are *Not*.

– p. 196

_____

_____

_____

_____

_____

_____

_____

_____

_____

_____

_____

_____

_____

October 31

A worldwide government would level the playing field—
and this idea, while driving to the core of the debate
regarding basic human dignity, is anathema to the
world's "haves," who want the "have-nots" to go seek
their *own* fortune—ignoring, of course, the fact that the
"haves" *control* all that others would seek.

– p. 197

_____

_____

_____

_____

_____

_____

_____

_____

_____

_____

_____

_____

_____

November 1

So the real job, and the first job in restructuring the social order, is to make sure each person and each nation has equal *opportunity*.

– p. 197

_____

_____

_____

_____

_____

_____

_____

_____

_____

_____

_____

_____

_____

November 2

Revolutions and civil wars are inevitable, as are wars between nations, so long as the "haves" continue seeking to exploit the "have-nots" under the guise of providing *opportunity.*

November 3

No one's point of view is less worthy of being heard
than another's; No one human being has less dignity
than another.

– p. 200

_____

_____

_____

_____

_____

_____

_____

_____

_____

_____

_____

_____

_____

November 4

The incentive to succeed, to make the most of one's life, should not be economic or materialistic reward ... When the incentive for greatness is not economic—when economic security and basic materialistic needs are guaranteed to all—then incentive will not disappear, but be of a different sort, *increasing* in strength and determination, producing *true* greatness ... .

– p. 200

_____

_____

_____

_____

_____

_____

_____

_____

_____

_____

_____

_____

_____

_____

November 5

If you define "better" as *bigger, better, more* money, power, sex, and *stuff* (houses, cars, clothes, CD collections—whatever)... and if you define "life" as the period elapsing between birth and death in this your present existence, then you're doing nothing to get out of the trap that has *created* your planet's predicament.

– p. 201

_____

_____

_____

_____

_____

_____

_____

_____

_____

_____

_____

_____

_____

_____

November 6

The incentive of most of humankind is to achieve, acquire, obtain *things*. Those who do not care about things let them go easily.

– p. 201

_____

_____

_____

_____

_____

_____

_____

_____

_____

_____

_____

_____

November 7

. . . this struggle becomes not a struggle at all, but a process
. . . a process of Self-definition (not self-discovery), of
Growth (not learning), of Being (not doing). The *reason* for
seeking, striving, searching, stretching, and *succeeding* becomes completely different. The reason for doing *anything*
is changed, and with it the doer is likewise changed. The
reason becomes the process, and the doer becomes a be-er.

– p. 202

_____

_____

_____

_____

_____

_____

_____

_____

_____

_____

_____

_____

_____

_____

November 8

For all the world's magnificence, you have not found a way to be magnificent enough to stop people from starving to death, much less stop killing each other. You actually let *children* starve to death right in front of you. You actually kill people because they disagree with you.

– p. 204-205

November 9

The first mark of a primitive society is that it thinks itself advanced. The first mark of a primitive consciousness is that it thinks itself enlightened.

– p. 205

_____

_____

_____

_____

_____

_____

_____

_____

_____

_____

_____

_____

_____

. . . you cannot earn your way into God's good graces, and you do not have to, because you are already there. This is something you cannot accept, because it is something you cannot *give*. When you learn to *give* unconditionally (which is to say, *love* unconditionally), then will you learn to *receive* unconditionally.

– p. 207

_____

_____

_____

_____

_____

_____

_____

_____

_____

_____

_____

_____

_____

November 11

People have a right to basic survival. Even if they do *nothing*. Even if they contribute *nothing*. Survival with dignity is one of the basic rights of life. I have given you enough resources to be able to guarantee that to everyone. All you have to do is share.

— p. 207

_____

_____

_____

_____

_____

_____

_____

_____

_____

_____

_____

_____

_____

November 12

It is not for you to judge the journey of another's soul.
It is for you to decide who YOU are, not who another
has been or has failed to be.

— p. 208

_____

_____

_____

_____

_____

_____

_____

_____

_____

_____

_____

_____

November 13

Envy is a natural emotion urging you to strive to be more. It is the two-year-old child yearning and urging herself to reach that doorknob which her big brother can reach. There is nothing wrong with that. There is nothing wrong with envy. It is a motivator. It is pure desire. It gives birth to greatness.

– p. 209

November 14

Jealousy, on the other hand, is a fear-driven emotion making one willing for the other to have less. It is an emotion often based in bitterness. It proceeds from anger and leads to anger. And it kills. Jealousy can kill. Anyone who's been in a jealous triangle knows that.

– p. 209

_____

_____

_____

_____

_____

_____

_____

_____

_____

_____

_____

_____

_____

November 15

Those who are envious will be given every opportunity to succeed in *their* own way. No one will be held back economically, politically, socially. Not by reason of race, gender or sexual orientation. Not by reason of birth, class status or age. Nor for any reason at all. Discrimination for *any* reason will simply no longer be tolerated.

– p. 209-210

_____

_____

_____

_____

_____

_____

_____

_____

_____

_____

_____

_____

_____

_____

_____

November 16

The human spirit rises; it does not fall in the face of true opportunity. The soul seeks a higher experience of itself, not a lower. Anyone who has experienced *true magnificence*, if only for a moment, knows this.

– p. 211

_____

_____

_____

_____

_____

_____

_____

_____

_____

_____

_____

_____

November 17

The guidance you are getting is to *follow your heart.*
Listen to your *soul.* Hear your *self.* Even when I present
you with an option, an idea, a point of view, you are
under no obligation to accept that as your own. If you
disagree, then *disagree.*

– p. 215

_____

_____

_____

_____

_____

_____

_____

_____

_____

_____

_____

_____

_____

_____

November 18

. . . you are the Highest Source.

– p. 215

_____

_____

_____

_____

_____

_____

_____

_____

_____

_____

_____

_____

_____

_____

November 19

Remember, it's always your *new thought* that creates your reality. Always.

– p. 215

_____

_____

_____

_____

_____

_____

_____

_____

_____

_____

_____

_____

_____

_____

November 20

Joy at the work place had nothing to do with function, and everything to do with purpose.

– p. 217

_____

_____

_____

_____

_____

_____

_____

_____

_____

_____

_____

_____

_____

November 21

The resources of your planet—*including* the *fruits of the labors* of the masses of the indescribably poor who are continually and systematically exploited—belong to all the world's people, not just those who are rich and powerful enough to do the exploiting.

— p. 220

_____

_____

_____

_____

_____

_____

_____

_____

_____

_____

_____

_____

_____

November 22

God is *everything*, and God *becomes* everything.

_____

_____

_____

_____

_____

_____

_____

_____

_____

_____

_____

_____

_____

_____

November 23

Know that every thought I am sending you, you are receiving through the filter of your own experience, of your own truth, of your own understandings, and of your own decisions, choices, and declarations about Who You Are and Who You Choose to Be. There's no other way you can receive it. There's no other way you should.

— p. 223

November 24

. . . My decision from the beginning has been to give you the freedom to create your life—and hence, your Self—as you wish to *be*. You cannot know your Self as the Creator if I tell you what to create, how to create, and then force, require, or cause you to do so.

– p. 224

. . . the struggle between the "haves" and the "have-nots" has been going on forever and is epidemic on your planet. It will ever be thus so long as economic interests, rather than humanitarian interests, run the world—so long as man's body, and not man's soul, is man's highest concern.

– p. 227

November 26

Truth and God are found in the same place: in the silence. When you have found God, and when you have found truth, it is not necessary to talk about it. It is self-evident.

– p. 232

_____

_____

_____

_____

_____

_____

_____

_____

_____

_____

_____

_____

_____

November 27

You teach what you choose to learn.

– p. 232

_____

_____

_____

_____

_____

_____

_____

_____

_____

_____

_____

_____

_____

_____

November 28

Your future is creatable. Create it as you want it.

– p. 235

_____

_____

_____

_____

_____

_____

_____

_____

_____

_____

_____

_____

_____

. . . the Eternal Moment of Now is also *forever changing*. It is like a mosaic—one that is always there, but constantly shifting. You can't blink, because it will be different when you open your eyes again.

— p. 235-236

November 30

Sometimes the change in the All is subtle, virtually indiscernible, depending upon the power of the *thought*. But when there is an intense thought—or a *collective thought*—then there is *tremendous* impact, incredible effect.

– p. 236

_____

_____

_____

_____

_____

_____

_____

_____

_____

_____

_____

_____

_____

December 1

You must learn to live within the contradiction. And you must understand the greatest truth: Nothing Matters.

– p. 236

_____

_____

_____

_____

_____

_____

_____

_____

_____

_____

_____

_____

December 2

The process of shifting the consciousness, increasing the spiritual awareness, of an entire planet, is a slow process. It takes time and great patience. Lifetimes. Generations. Yet slowly you are coming around. Gently you are shifting. Quietly, there is change.

– p. 239

_____

_____

_____

_____

_____

_____

_____

_____

_____

_____

_____

_____

December 3

Wisdom which comes from within is not nearly so easily discarded as wisdom which comes from another.

— p. 239

_____

_____

_____

_____

_____

_____

_____

_____

_____

_____

_____

_____

_____

_____

December 4

You are being given the opportunity to live out your own destiny. Your own consciousness will create the result.

— p. 240

_____

_____

_____

_____

_____

_____

_____

_____

_____

_____

_____

_____

_____

December 5

What you fear is what you will draw to you. What you resist, persists. What you look at disappears—giving you a chance to recreate it all over again, if you wish, or banish it forever from your experience. What you choose, you experience.

— p. 240

_____

_____

_____

_____

_____

_____

_____

_____

_____

_____

_____

_____

December 6

Never see yourself again as separate from one another, and never see yourself as separate from Me. Never tell anything but the whole truth to anyone, and never again accept anything less than *your* grandest truth about Me.

– p. 242

_____

_____

_____

_____

_____

_____

_____

_____

_____

_____

_____

_____

_____

December 7

. . . when you see and understand that you are One with Everyone, you can *not* tell an untruth or withhold important data or be anything but totally visible with all others *because you will be clear that it is in your own best interests to do so.*

– p. 242

_____

_____

_____

_____

_____

_____

_____

_____

_____

_____

_____

_____

_____

December 8

. . . you will not have, cannot produce, the society for which you have always yearned and of which you have always dreamed unless and until you see with wisdom and clarity the ultimate truth: that what you do to others, you do to yourself; what you fail to do for others, you fail to do for yourself; that the pain of others is your pain, and the joy of others your joy . . .

_____

_____

_____

_____

_____

_____

_____

_____

_____

_____

_____

_____

_____

_____

December 9

And when you are thus totally enlightened—that is, once more filled with the light—you may even choose, as your particular reason for returning to physical life, the re-minding of others.

– p. 243

_____

_____

_____

_____

_____

_____

_____

_____

_____

_____

_____

_____

_____

December 10

We are always united, you and I. We cannot *not* be.

– p. 243

_____

_____

_____

_____

_____

_____

_____

_____

_____

_____

_____

_____

_____

December 11

It is also possible to live in the physical body in conscious union with All That Is; in conscious awareness of *ultimate truth*; in conscious expression of Who You Really Are. When you do this, you serve as a model for all others, others who are living in forgetfulness. You become a living re-minder. And in this you save others from becoming permanently lost in their forgetfulness.

– p. 243

_____

_____

_____

_____

_____

_____

_____

_____

_____

_____

_____

_____

_____

December 12

Yet what makes you think those spirits—those Holy Spirits—cannot, or would not choose to, live elsewhere in the universe, *just as they did when they came to your world*?

– p. 245

_____

_____

_____

_____

_____

_____

_____

_____

_____

_____

_____

_____

_____

December 13

Everything—*everything—that ever was, is now, and ever will be exists right now.* And so, all that is . . . Is. Yet all that IS is constantly *changing,* for life is an *ongoing process of creation.* Therefore, in a very real sense, That Which IS . . . IS NOT.

– p. 246

_____

_____

_____

_____

_____

_____

_____

_____

_____

_____

_____

_____

December 14

. . . in order for organized religion to succeed, it has to make people believe they *need* it. In order for people to put faith in something else, they must first lose faith in themselves.

– p. 247

_____

_____

_____

_____

_____

_____

_____

_____

_____

_____

_____

_____

_____

December 15

If you question, you start to think! If you think, you start to go back to that Source Within.

_____

_____

_____

_____

_____

_____

_____

_____

_____

_____

_____

_____

_____

December 16

Any clear thinker who looks at what religion has done *must* assume religion has no God! For it is religion which has filled the hearts of men with fear of God, where once man loved That Which Is in all its splendor.

– p. 248

_____

_____

_____

_____

_____

_____

_____

_____

_____

_____

_____

_____

_____

December 17

God is *not* above man, and man is *not* above woman—
that is *not* the "natural order of things"—but it *is* the
way everyone who had power (namely, men) *wished* it
was when they formed their male-worship religions,
systematically editing out half the material from their
final version of the "holy scriptures" and twisting the
rest to fit the mold of their male model of the world.

– p. 248

December 18

You are *all* priests. *Every single one of you.*

– p. 249

_____

_____

_____

_____

_____

_____

_____

_____

_____

_____

_____

_____

_____

_____

December 19

There is no one person or class of people more "suited" to do My work than any other.

– p. 249

_____

_____

_____

_____

_____

_____

_____

_____

_____

_____

_____

_____

_____

December 20

God's greatest gift is the sharing of God's power. *I would have you be like Me.*

– p. 249

_____

_____

_____

_____

_____

_____

_____

_____

_____

_____

_____

_____

_____

December 21

You have been made in the Image and Likeness of God—it is that destiny you came to fulfill. You did not come here to strive and to struggle and to never "get there." Nor did I send you on a mission impossible to complete.

December 22

I have said, "God is everything, and God *becomes* everything. There is nothing which God is not, and all that God is experiencing of Itself, God is experiencing in, as, and through you." In My purest form, I am the Absolute. I am Absolutely Everything, and therefore, I need, want, and demand absolutely nothing.

– p. 249

_____

_____

_____

_____

_____

_____

_____

_____

_____

_____

_____

_____

_____

December 23

From this absolutely pure form, I am as you make Me. . . . Yet, no matter what you make of Me, I cannot forget, and will always return to, My Purest Form. All the rest is a fiction. It is something you are *making up*.

— p. 249-250

_____

_____

_____

_____

_____

_____

_____

_____

_____

_____

_____

_____

_____

_____

December 24

. . . who could be jealous when one has, and *is*,
Everything?

– p. 250

_____

_____

_____

_____

_____

_____

_____

_____

_____

_____

_____

_____

_____

December 25

You and I *are* one—both now and forever more. Go now, and make of your life a statement of this truth.

– p. 250

_____

_____

_____

_____

_____

_____

_____

_____

_____

_____

_____

_____

_____

December 26

There are those who would make Me a vengeful God;
but on whom would I take vengeance, since all that
exists is Me? And why would I punish Myself for simply
creating?

– p. 250

_____

_____

_____

_____

_____

_____

_____

_____

_____

_____

_____

_____

_____

December 27

. . . if you must think of us as separate, why would I create you, give *you* the power to create, give you the freedom of choice to create what you wish to experience, then punish you forever for making the "wrong" choice? I tell you this: I would not do such a thing—and in that truth lies your freedom from the tyranny of God . . . In truth, there *is* no tyranny—except in your imagination.

– p. 250

_____

_____

_____

_____

_____

_____

_____

_____

_____

_____

_____

_____

_____

December 28

You may come home whenever you wish. We can be together again whenever you want. The ecstasy of your union with Me is yours to know again. At the drop of a hat. At the feel of the wind on your face. At the sound of a cricket under diamond skies on a summer night.

— p. 250

December 29

I am with you always, even unto the end of time. Your union with Me is complete—it always was, always is, and always will be.

— p. 250

_____

_____

_____

_____

_____

_____

_____

_____

_____

_____

_____

_____

_____

_____

December 30

Cause your days and nights to be reflections of the highest idea within you. Allow your moments of Now to be filled with the spectacular ecstasy of God make manifest through you. Do it through the expression of your Love, eternal and unconditional, for all those whose lives you touch.

— p. 251

December 31

Be a light unto the darkness, and curse it not. Be a bringer of the light.

– p. 251

_____

_____

_____

_____

_____

_____

_____

_____

_____

_____

_____

_____

_____

_____

ABOUT THE CONVERSATIONS WITH GOD SERIES:

Conversations with God has become one of the most compelling series of books in modern publishing, with over 1.5 million hardcovers sold of Books 1 and 2, and translations into 24 languages to date. Neale Donald Walsch has presented a concept of God we can understand and accept, a God who answers clearly all the questions we have wanted to ask, about all the subjects that are fundamental to us — life and death, love and hate, good and evil, heaven and hell, the meaning of the soul — a God who makes sense, and gives us hope. You will find these books to be among the most important you will ever read, a new paradigm for human life and our relationship to the universe. *Book 1* was originally published in trade paperback by Hampton Roads, but is now available in hardcover from Penguin-Putnam in New York (ISBN 0-399-14278-9, $19.95).

From Hampton Roads:

Conversations with God, Book 2
Neale Donald Walsch

The dialogue continues in this anxiously-awaited follow-up to the fastest-selling book in the company's history. *Conversations with God, Book 2* resumes the dialogue where *Book 1* left off, moving from personal issues to more global and political concerns. Included are questions about the nature of time and space and human sexuality, as well as geophysical and geopolitical considerations of worldwide implication. The dialogue in *Book 2* is, in Neale Donald Walsch's own words, ". . .captivating, disturbing, and challenging. . . .In this book, God suggests nothing less than a social, sexual, political, and economic revolution that would help create the paradise on Earth we all seek." Just as fascinating and compelling as *Book 1*, *Conversations with God, Book 2* will take you to new and more expansive understandings, to greater and more universal truths—until, of course, The Dialogue Expands. . .

5½ x 8 ¼ hardcover, 288 pages, ISBN 1-57174-056-2, $19.95

Conversations with God, Book 1 Guidebook
Neale Donald Walsch

The success of *Conversations with God, Book 1* is even greater than anyone imagined! Church and individual study groups have formed all over the nation, and many have written to the author, requesting that he create a workbook to help guide them through the material. Walsch has responded to the demand and has created the *Conversations with God, Book 1 Guidebook*—a step-by-step guide and exercise manual for those seeking to apply the truths in Book 1 to their daily lives. Whether it be for practical application or just to further one's understanding of the dialogue, the *Conversations with God, Book 1 Guidebook* is an excellent and indispensable aid. It is written so that people who have not even read the other books can still understand and work with the concepts.

6 x 9 trade paper, 216 pages, ISBN 1-57174-048-1, $12.95

In Closing

Since receiving the information contained in this book, and quietly spreading the word about it, I have answered many inquiries, both about how it was received and about the dialogue itself. I honor every inquiry, and the sincerity with which it is made. People simply want to know more about this, and that is understandable.

While I wish I could take every phone call and personally respond to every letter, it is just not possible to do that. Among other things, I would be spending a great deal of time answering essentially the same questions over and over again. So I've thought about how I could interact with you more efficiently, and still honor each inquiry.

I decided to write a monthly letter to those with questions or comments regarding this dialogue. In this way it is possible for me to respond to all the inquiries which come in and to react to all the commentaries, without having to write many, many individual letters each month. I know this may not be the best way to communicate with you, and it certainly is not the most personal, but it is what I am now capable of doing.

The monthly letter is available upon request to:

ReCreation
Postal Drawer 3547
Central Point, Oregon 97502

In the beginning this letter was made available at no fee, but we never dreamed so many would ask for it. Because of the mounting costs, we are now asking for a minimal donation of twenty-five dollars per year so that we can continue to reach as many people as possible. If you are unable financially to help us with these costs, please ask for a scholarship subscription.

I'm glad you have been able to share this extraordinary dialogue with me. I wish you the highest experience of life's rich blessings, and an awareness of God in your life that brings you peace, joy, and love through all your days and endeavors.

Neale Donald Walsch

ABOUT NEALE DONALD WALSCH

Neale Donald Walsch lives with his wife, Nancy, in southern Oregon. Together they have formed ReCreation, a non-profit foundation for personal growth and spiritual understanding, with the goal of giving people back to themselves. Walsch lectures and hosts workshops throughout the country to support and spread the messages contained in the *Conversations with God* series.

For a limited edition reprint of the original cover painting by Louis Jones, please write to:

The Louis & Susan Jones Art Gallery
Dominion Tower, Suite 105
999 Waterside Drive
Norfolk, Virginia 23510

Or call (757) 625-6505 for further information.

Hampton Roads Publishing Company
publishes and distributes books on a variety of subjects,
including metaphysics, health, complementary medicine,
visionary fiction, and other related topics.

To order or receive a copy of our latest catalog, call toll-free,
(800) 766-8009, or send your name and address to:

Hampton Roads Publishing Company, Inc.
134 Burgess Lane
Charlottesville, VA 22902